400
mus

ENGLISH ELECTRIC
TRACTION ALBUM

John Glover

LONDON

IAN ALLAN LTD

Contents

First published 1981

ISBN 0 7110 1059 5

Published by Ian Allan Ltd, Shepperton, Surrey; and printed by Ian Allan Printing Ltd at their works at Coombelands in Runnymede, England

Introduction

The name of The English Electric Co Ltd cannot be divorced from the motive power of British Rail today. Although formed in 1918 by merger, it was the incorporation of the companies of D. Napier and Son, Vulcan Foundry, and Robert Stephenson and Hawthorn, later joined by W. H. Dorman and W. G. Bagnall which gave English Electric such a prominent place in the supply of equipment to the world's railways. Nowhere was this more apparent than in Britain; besides developing a highly successful range of diesel engines, deliveries of which took place from the 1930s onwards, English Electric was also extremely active in the electric traction field.

The firm's golden opportunity for home sales came with the 1955 Modernisation Plan. English Electric were awarded contracts for supplying complete locomotives in each of the diesel power classes, and in all but one case the results were outstandingly successful. At the same time, construction of English Electric powered diesel shunters proceeded apace, and power equipments were manufactured for the Southern's fleet of diesel-electric multiple-units. Orders also encompassed both ac and dc electric locomotives and the electro-diesels, and traction motors were supplied for a wide

variety of electric multiple-units. Even the Type 2 power range of diesel locomotives came to be associated with the firm through a contract for the supply of new engines for the Class 31 locomotives from 1964 onwards. Finally, the technically advanced Class 50 emerged in 1967; shortly afterwards the identity of English Electric was lost as the firm became part of the GEC/AEI combine.

English Electric always specialised in the provision of locomotives designed to suit the requirements of individual customers, whilst at the same time providing a considerable measure of component standardisation. For example, by using a common 10in cylinder bore and 12in stroke, a wide range of diesel engine power output was achieved with a high degree of component interchangeability. The engines themselves came in two forms — the vertical 'in line' engines as used in the diesel shunters and all Southern Region applications, and the space saving 'V-form' design used elsewhere except in the 'Deltics'. Those used on British Rail are as follows:

Class	Engine	hp
08, 09, 13	6KT	350
201-7	4SRKT MkII	500/600
73/0,73/1	4SRKT MkII	600
20	8SVT MkII	1,000
31	12SVT	1,470
37	12CSVT	1,750
40	16SVT MkII	2,000
50	16CSVT	2,700
55	Napier-Deltic 18-25	1,650

The Initial figure represents the number of cylinders in the engine; C indicates charge-cooled; S is supercharged; (R)K is an 'in line' engine; V is the V-form engine, and T indicates a traction application. Thus the Class 37 has a 12-cylinder charge-cooled supercharged V-form engine for traction.

The sheer volume of the firm's output meant that British Rail placed great reliance upon English Electric. Over half the diesel-electric locomotive fleet in 1967 was English Electric built or powered, and Southern Region electric multiple-units had been exclusively using English Electric power equipments since 1936. Today, the lapse of time since their con-

struction puts all the firm's products at least into their middle age, whilst some of the early diesel locomotives will shortly achieve a quarter century of service. Yet, prototypes apart, class withdrawals have been confined to the 10 Class 23 'Baby Deltics' and the 24 Southern Region Class 71 electric loco-motives, 10 of which had been converted to Class 74 electro-diesels. Whilst it is perhaps still too early to judge the products of the company as a whole, it can be safely said that the designs were technically sound and backed by a wealth of experience, even if they were of a generally conservative nature. Above all, *they worked*. Indeed, the expertise remains with GEC Traction Ltd, and the Class 56 freight locomotives are powered by a descendent of the V16 engine.

Turning now to the present volume, it seemed that the contribution of English Electric had been allowed to go largely unremarked for too long, and this album is an attempt to redress the balance. It is not a technical book. The subject is the photo-graphic portrayal of the products of the Trac-tion Division of the former English Electric Company which were still in service at the end of the 1970s. A short introduction precedes each of the classes, which appear in the approximate chronological order of their con-struction.

All photographs in this book are the work of members of the Phoenix Railway Photographic Circle, a group whose interest is the furtherance of the art of photography of all forms of modern rail traction. We hope that you, the reader, enjoy it.

I would like to thank Mike Scott of GEC Traction Ltd for so patiently answering my queries, and the librarians of the Chartered Institute of Transport and the Institution of Mechanical Engineers for unearthing much relevant literature. Brian Webb's book *English Electric Main Line Diesel Locomotives of British Rail* provided a particularly useful reference, as did a whole host of contemporary articles in the various railway periodicals.

Ewell, Surrey　　　　　　　　　　　*John Glover*
January 1980

4

Class 502:
Southport Electric Units

The Liverpool-Southport electric services operate on the 630V dc third-rail system, and the Class 502 units were ordered by the London Midland and Scottish Railway. They were delivered from 1939 onwards. English Electric provided the traction motors, and four of these 235hp units are contained in each of the Motor Open Brake Seconds which weigh no more than a modest 42 tons for their 66ft 6in overall length. The trailer cars weigh only 24-25 tons. Air-operated sliding doors are fitted, and train formations are officially three cars — although formerly other combinations were frequently seen. Amongst the oldest passenger vehicles on British Rail, these veterans were being superseded at the end of the 1970s after a 40-year working life.

Below: A two-car formation of 'Southport' stock leaves the decaying remains of Liverpool Exchange station with the 11.44 for Ormskirk on 23 September 1976. *Brian Morrison*

Above: Two years later, and the Southport and Ormskirk trains have gained access to the underground Liverpool Central station. This is the scene at about 10.45 on 23 August 1978. *Peter Shoesmith*

Left: The approach to Southport on the same day, seen looking over the top of two units stabled on the former Crossens extension. Both have been repainted in the blue and grey livery, and carry the Merseyside PTE logo as well as that of British Rail. *Peter Shoesmith*

Above right: Outside Southport station on 23 June 1979, newcomer No 507.022 is stabled alongside a Class 502 unit, whilst a further Class 502 approaches. *Les Nixon*

Right: Southport station, formerly Chapel Street, boasts a fine overall roof; the train is about to depart for Liverpool. Although these units have sliding doors, the guard retains a swing door which, most unusually, opens outwards. *Les Nixon*

Classes 08, 09 and 13:
Diesel Shunters

Dieselisation in Britain started with the shunting locomotive. Following experiments conducted by the London Midland and Scottish Railway, the English Electric 6K engine first appeared in a shunting locomotive built by the Hawthorn Leslie subsidiary. It was subsequently sold to the LMS and remained in capital stock until withdrawn as No 12002 in 1956.

All the 'Big Four' railways took up the idea, and it was the Southern Railway which developed the practice of itself building the mechanical parts but purchasing the remainder. Meanwhile, the LMS had concluded that a six-cylinder engine of 300-350hp was required, and electric transmission was favoured. The latter avoided time-consuming gear changing, and was proof against careless driving; indeed it was possible to reverse the driving torque before the locomotive came to rest without causing damage.

English Electric listed the features that they saw as desirable attributes in a heavy shunting locomotive:

(1) High tractive effort at starting and at low speeds.
(2) Adequate fuel capacity for continuous operation over lengthy periods without refuelling.
(3) Robust design and construction, reducing maintenance to a minimum, and maximum accessibility to working parts.
(4) Extra torque at starting, enabling the locomotive to exert the maximum tractive effort compatible with its adhesive weight.

The scene was thus set for the emergence of the standard British Rail diesel shunter in 1952. In the ensuing 10 years, a total of 1,193 units were completed, all but 171 having English Electric engines and traction motors. The railway workshops at Crewe, Darlington, Derby, Doncaster and Horwich constructed the locomotives which are fitted with the 6KT engine which was by now developing 350hp at 630rev/min. Two nose-suspended and force-ventilated traction motors provide the drive through double reduction gears. Each locomotive weighs 49 tons and has driving wheels of 4ft 6in diameter; the maximum speed is 20mph for the standard Class 08 version, although the Southern Region Class 09 variant is geared for a top speed of 27mph.

Within its 29ft 4in overall length and 11ft 6in wheelbase, perfection seems to have been achieved. In a 1969 opinion 'it is well loved, proven, reliable — seems to be unbeatable and no possible advantage can be forseen for ever changing it'. Ten years later, over 900 remained in service.

Variations are few, but in 1965 six locomotives were converted at Darlington into 'master and slave' locomotives for hump shunting at the newly opened Tinsley marshalling yard. The cab of the 'slave' was removed, and ballast added to assist adhesion, bringing the total weight of the pair up to 120 tons.

Above right: Smartly turned out No 08.944 is guided into the dmu depot at Southall on 18 October 1979. *John Glover*

Right: On 5 March 1979, No 08.817 uses its 350hp to haul a Kittybrewster to Ferryhill trip freight through the northern approaches to Aberdeen. *Brian Morrison*

Left: At Ferryhill, No 08.515 is seen marshalling Post Office vans after turning these single-sided vehicles on the turntable on 3 September 1977. Through careful control of platforming arrangements, it has since proved possible to largely dispense with the chore of turning the vans at the end of each trip. *Les Nixon*

Below left: No 08.868 works a few empties up the overgrown line to the exchange sidings with Tube Investments Ltd, Chesterfield on 7 June 1979. *Kevin Lane*

Right: A short train of steel scrap passes Masboro' Station South box at Rotherham headed by No 08.223 on 16 May 1977. *Geoff Dowling*

Below: One of the three 'master and slave' pairs of diesel shunters, No 13.002, is seen propelling wagons over the hump at Tinsley yard, Sheffield, on 20 September 1976. The locomotives were originally intended to work 'back to back', but the present arrangement was found to be more satisfactory. *Les Nixon*

Left: Ordinary shunters also find work at Tinsley, but not on a Sunday. Having their Sunday rest on 26 September 1976 are Nos 08.335, 08.024 and 08.507. *Philip Hawkins*

Below left: No 08.534 draws a trainload of Ford cars on to the main line at Allerton Junction, Liverpool on 28 June 1978. The train engine is already attached to the rear. *David Flitcroft*

Right: Night-time at New Street, Birmingham in February 1979, as No 08.908 waits to attach some vans to an incoming train. *Geoff Dowling*

Below: The rebuilt Peterborough station on 13 July 1976 sees No 08.438 crossing from the down side sidings on to the down main line. *Les Nixon*

Left: On a fine summer's day in 1978, No 08.228 runs 'wrong line' through Manningtree during a permanent way possession. *John Howie*

Below: Passengers waiting for their London train seem oblivious of the Class 08 shunter and its train of Freightliner flat wagons passing through Ipswich on 2 March 1979. *Michael Baker*

Right: The Silvertown Tramway in East London produces little rail traffic nowadays, but No 08.269 has found a few wagon loads of scrap to take back to Temple Mills yard. The train is seen at Silvertown on 30 August 1979. *John Glover*

Below right: Agricultural produce features in the rail traffic of East Anglia. No 08.716 was photographed near Bury St Edmunds on 16 March 1978; the eight Covhops contain sugar from the British Sugar Corporation, and there is grain from Associated British Maltsters in the two privately owned vehicles. *John Baker*

Left: A beautiful day by the seaside sees no sign of work for No 08.895. This was the scene at Penzance on 16 July 1978. *Brian Morrison*

Top: The Class 09 shunters are all allocated to the Southern Region. No 09.019, the Tilmanstone Colliery branch locomotive, waits at Shepherds Well as 4CEP unit No 7158 approaches with the 11.40 from Victoria on 22 April 1976. *Wyn Hobson*

Above: Sold out of service by British Rail, Class 08 locomotive No 3101 found a new home at the Loughborough depot of the Amey Roadstone Corporation, where it was photographed on 30 September 1976. *Kevin Lane*

Classes 201-207:
Southern's Diesel-Electric Units

The decrepit nature of the Hastings line rolling stock in the early 1950s had led to pressures for its replacement, and in 1955 32 locomotive-hauled coaches were ordered. These were put in hand on short 56ft 11in underframes, their length being dictated by the limited platform capacity at Charing Cross. Before delivery however, the decision to dieselise as an interim measure was taken as electrification could not take place until 1963! Accordingly, the vehicles under construction were converted to five six-car units and a further two units were ordered. Conversion required the fitting of electric heating, through control cables and the electro-pneumatic brake. The first 6S unit (later Class 201) entered service on 6 May 1957.

Power in the new units was provided by an English Electric 4SRKT Mk II engine mounted above the floor in each of the two end vehicles, and of which the Southern had had good reports from the Egyptian State Railways where it had been in use since 1947. The engine delivered 500hp at 850rev/min; transmission was by way of two nose-suspended traction motors as used in emu stock. These were mounted on the inner end bogies to help balance the axle loadings. Each motor coach carries 340 gallons of fuel, which is enough for 14 hours continuous running or a distance of about 800 miles.

At the design stage, thought was given to arranging the equipment in a similar manner to an electro-diesel so that 750V dc could be taken from the third-rail between London and Tonbridge. However, additional equipment was needed, and it was concluded that the complication was not financially justified. It would also have been quite practicable to remove the diesel generator set had electrification take place — an event which today seems as far away as ever.

Subsequent orders from unit No 1011 onwards were on the standard length underframe, as no provision was now necessary for a locomotive. These were designated 6L (Class 202). The capacity of a six-car unit was thus raised from 242 seats to 288 by incorporating an additional seating bay in each vehicle. Underframes and bogies came from Ashford, and the bodies and interiors from Eastleigh. Buffet cars for the 6B/Class 203 units were built at Lancing. Due to the size of the diesel engine, it was impractical to construct a passenger gangway alongside it. Through communication was thus not possible between sets, and passengers who wished to make use of the buffet car in a 12-car formation had to take care where they joined the train. All buffet facilities were withdrawn from mid-1980.

The critics were scathing about the appearance. 'Externally at least it has nowhere beautified the railway scene. The slab sides have obviously been dictated by the restricted clearances of the Hastings line, but to combine them with the standard front end of a modern SR suburban electric unit and produce a drabber box on wheels than anything yet turned out by BR cannot have been equally inescapable . . . This is the nadir.' Thus spake *Trains Illustrated*. Performance, fortunately, was more satisfactory, and the target of a 90min London-Hastings timing was achieved with ease within the maximum permitted speed of 75mph.

Also constructed in 1957 were a number of two-car 2H sets (Class 204) for local services in Hampshire, the Hastings area and Berkshire. These units quickly became popular with the public and an intermediate trailer was soon ordered for all but four of these units to increase their seating capacity. Initially the same 4SRKT Mk II engine was fitted, but the additional trailer made the units under-powered. Accordingly, an uprated 600hp engine was ordered, the redundant 500hp engines being transferred to the six-car trains then in course of delivery. The new 3H (Class 205) three-car units achieved a fuel consumption of 2.5 miles per gallon. The appearance of these sets closely resembles the 2HAP electric units, and indeed the control trailers of each are virtually identical.

The Southern's preference for diesel-electric multiple-units persisted with the delivery from Eastleigh of No 1301, first of the 'East Sussex' three-car 3D/Class 207 units on 4 April 1962. Electric transmission fitted in well with the fleet of electric multiple-units; as with compressed air braking and electrical control, it was standard SR practice. And although the large medium-speed diesel engine and generator was bulky, it was also rugged and required little maintenance. These units also received the 600hp version of the 4SRKT Mk II.

An attempt was made to tidy up the front end design, and the jumper cables were recessed in the fibreglass cab front, with the whole having a cleaner finish. Technically, there was little change, although the refinement of wheelslip protection was fitted.

Changing traffic conditions led to a re-formation of some of the Class 201 sets in 1964. One result was the appearance of six units utilising two narrow Hastings line vehicles and one redundant EPB driving trailer. Officially 3R/Class 206, they were universally known as 'Tadpoles' and worked the Reading-Tonbridge line until their replacement in 1979 by Western Region dmus. A seating capacity of 140 (second class only) was provided, but more often than not the non-gangwayed EPB trailer was locked out of use due to collector-guard working. These units were not however withdrawn; the EPB trailers have been used to augment the remaining Class 204 sets to three cars, and the Hastings vehicles have been repainted blue and grey to match the Class 201 units.

Despite obvious problems such as the diesel engines taking up valuable space which could have been used for seating, the decision of the Southern to use diesel-electric power seems to have been vindicated. The availability of the dmu fleet has been exemplary, with 93% being regularly achieved, together with 90,000-120,000 miles per casualty, or less than one failure per engine per year. Barring the few Hampshire units at Eastleigh, all are based at St Leonards. Heavy overhaul is carried out at Swindon.

Right: Class 203 Buffet unit No 1033 leaves Charing Cross — still emblazoned with the initials of the Southern Railway — for Hastings. The cramped nature of the station is apparent in this view taken on 14 September 1977. *Brian Morrison*

Above: A pair of Hastings express units speed through Crowhurst on 16 October 1978. Class 201 unit No 1006 is constructed on the short underframes, and the power cars have only three compartments each. The roof hatch allows the engine to be removed for overhaul. *John Glover*

Left: The limited clearances on the Hastings line can be seen in this view through the overbridge at Tonbridge station, which leaves one in no doubt as to why the vehicles have slab sides! Class 202 unit No 1011 enters the station with a London-bound train on 16 October 1978. *John Glover*

Above right: The Class 205 units work regularly on Victoria-Uckfield services. No 1106 enters the country junction station of Eridge, also on 16 October 1978. The black diamond indicates that the leading vehicle (the Motor Open Brake Second) has luggage space. *John Glover*

Right: The Portsmouth-Southampton local services are exclusively in the hands of the Hampshire units. Class 205 unit No 1126 emerges from the tunnel at Southampton in June 1979. *Michael Baker*

Above: At St Denys, the line from Portsmouth joins the South Western main line. Class 205 unit No 1110 leaves the branch platforms on the last part of its run to Southampton in September 1975. *John Glover*

electrification, which extends here to give access to the car sheds on the right of the picture. *Peter Robinson*

Left: Class 207 unit No 1316 leaves Ore with a Hastings-Ashford train in 1972. Ore is the limit of third-rail

Below: Eridge in the spring. On 26 April 1979, Class 207 unit No 1312 leaves with an Uckfield-Victoria train, whilst sister unit No 1304 waits in the up loop with the connecting service to Tunbridge Wells. *John Glover*

Above: Hever station has lost its canopy but retains a signalbox on the down platform, jutting out from the booking office. Unit No 1306 is approaching with a southbound train, also on 26 April 1979. *John Glover*

Right: The unloved Class 206 'Tadpoles' got their name from their shape, which was due to the mixed ancestry of the vehicles. This March 1978 view shows unit No 1206 arriving in the double-sided platform at Guildford with the 08.04 Tonbridge-Reading. *John Glover*

24

Class 20:
English Electric Type 1

It fell to English Electric to deliver the first main line diesel locomotive ordered under the 1955 Modernisation Plan. Erected at Vulcan Foundry, No D8000 was handed over to British Rail on 3 June 1957. It was equipped with the Preston-built 8SVT MkII engine giving 1,000hp at 850rev/min and was supercharged by two Napier exhaust gas driven turbo-superchargers. This process increases the charge of air in the cylinders through compression, enabling more fuel to be burned and hence obtaining greater power from the engine. Four nose-suspended traction motors drive the wheels through single reduction spur gearing. Each locomotive has a fuel capacity of 400 gallons, which is sufficient for 300-500 miles running dependent upon the type of work performed.

Its delivery caused much interest, and a contemporary account enthused 'Every consideration has been given to the comfort of the locomotive crew ... there is even the refinement of a cooker'. On test, the Bo-Bo design did well; No D8000 was found to produce 76.2% of its output in the form of drawbar horsepower, the losses being due to the traction motors (101hp), auxiliaries (82hp), generators (43hp) and the locomotive's own resistance (12hp). It maintained 34.5mph up 1 in 200 with a 200ton passenger train and 18mph with a 500ton freight. A different kind of test concerned Nos D8010/11. In the early days of dieselisation, great concern was expressed about the toxicity of diesel fumes, and these two locomotives were seconded from Devons Road (Bow) to take part in top secret experiments in Lees Moor Tunnel on the ex-GNR Bradford-Keighley branch. Happily, the results were reassuring.

According to English Electric, the class was 'principally used for freight traffic but equally suitable for suburban passenger services'. The lack of a train heating boiler leads one to doubt this statement, although the 75mph maximum speed and their overall performance made them suitable in the summer months! This lack however doubtlessly contributed to the 90% availability rate; in 1966 the class was recorded as attaining 125,000 miles per casualty, which might be considered exceptional bearing in mind the relatively slow average speeds at which much of their work was being performed.

The original class of 20 locomotives was soon expanded, and by 1962 128 units had been delivered. Despite its proven ability, this design of locomotive was not chosen as standard in the Type 1 horsepower range; troubles with the replacement design soon manifested themselves however. A further order for 50 Class 20s followed in 1964, soon increased to 100. Of the total class of 228 locomotives, 135 were built at Vulcan Foundry, the balance of 93 being erected at the Robert Stephenson and Hawthorn works. Final deliveries took place nearly 11 years after the first, in itself something of a record.

'A robust machine with a very clean finish' was one comment on the original locomotives, which added that the marker lights and discs gave unity to the overall appearance. Deliveries from No D8128 onwards had the four character indicators substituted for the markers. Otherwise, the later locomotives are

25

all but identical to their predecessors, and there was disappointment in some circles that no attempt was made to uprate the engine. A minority were fitted with air brakes, and some Scottish Region examples have had the cabsides cut away to accommodate single line token apparatus. A few have slow-speed control.

As the trend to block trains progressed over the years, the requirement for a Bo-Bo of 73 tons diminished. Accordingly, the Class 20s tended to hunt in pairs with the cabs at the outer ends; this 2,000hp combination weighs only 13 tons more than a Class 40 and rests on the same number of wheels! At 93ft 7in however, it is 24ft 1in longer than its rival. Another reason for working the locomotives in multiple was the suggestion that the restricted visibility when working bonnet forward precluded single-manning.

The principal depots to which the Class 20s are allocated are Toton, Eastfield and Tinsley, with the balance at Haymarket and Immingham.

For a modest outlay, British Rail obtained a reliable fleet of locomotives of which the oldest has achieved nearly a quarter of a century's service. In view of the unsatisfactory nature of later designs which led to their premature withdrawal, the longevity of the Class 20s is a remarkable tribute to their designers and builders.

Right: Consecutively numbered Class 20s, Nos 20.145 and 20.144 leave Wath marshalling yard with an eastbound coal train on 26 April 1979.   *Les Nixon*

Below: 20.059 and 20.211 at Tinsley Station Junction, with the M1 viaduct and Blackburn Meadows power station in the background on 28 March 1977. *Chris Davis*

Left: The Conway Valley Centenary special from Crewe on 22 July 1979 was worked by a pair of Class 20s. Nos 20.153 and 20.165 are seen here approaching Roman Bridge. *John East*

Below: Nos 20.044 and 20.134 reverse a train of empties into the yard at Chinley station on 5 August 1977, prior to returning light to Toton. *Larry Goddard*

Right: No 20.093 at Scunthorpe with a transfer freight from Normanby Park on 4 September 1979. *Les Nixon*

Below right: On 15 June 1979, Nos 20.195 and 20.147 were photographed near Clay Cross with a trainload of coal bound for Toton yard. *Geoff Dowling*

Left: The sun catches No 20.194 working north out of Toton on 12 May 1976. *Geoff Dowling*

Below: Findern power station, Derbyshire, receives a train of coal supplies during a thunderstorm on 12 May 1976. Nos 20.051 and 20.053 are providing the power. *Geoff Dowling*

Right: Birch Coppice Colliery sidings, near Wilnecote, are shunted by Nos 20.066 and 20.174 on 4 December 1976. *Chris Davis*

Below right: Emerging from Manton Tunnel, Nos 20.198 and 20.193 take the Corby line at Manton Junction with a southbound freight on 23 August 1978. *Chris Davis*

Above: Nos 20.141 and 20.198 head a train of iron ore tippler empties past Sleaford East en route from Northampton to Boston on 14 June 1975.
Stanley Creer

Right: On 14 July 1979, Nos 20.134 and 20.139 work the 12.58 (SO) Skegness to Derby out of Boston on one of the few passenger trains diagrammed for Class 20 haulage. *Les Nixon*

Class 31:
Brush Type 2

Alone of the Type 2 locomotives, the A1A-A1A design built by Brush Traction suffered from six-wheeled bogies and consequently a weight of 109 tons. The first 20 of the class were delivered to the Eastern Region from 1957 as one of the pilot scheme orders; these locomotives differed from subsequent members of the class as they are fitted with electromagnetic control equipment and can only work in multiple with each other. These 80mph machines are identified by a red circle coupling code (and a nickname of 'Toffee Apples'!) and are classified as 31/0; all those remaining in traffic are allocated to Stratford. Opinions were divided on their appearance. In one view, the Class 31 was the most satisfactory visually of all the pilot scheme locomotives, particular approval being given to the way the front end doors were incorporated into the design. Others were more critical, seeing the recessing of the cab doors and windows as an unfortunate result of their conflicting with the roof curvature. This could have been avoided with a lower floor level for the cab.

Satisfactory performance led to further deliveries which had standard control gear and a top speed of 90mph. The class eventually totalled 263, the rating of the Mirlees engine having been successfully increased from 1,250hp to 1,365hp, 1,600hp and experimentally to 2,000hp. At one time the Brush Type 2 was almost synonymous with the dieselisation of East Anglia; it was only when deliveries reached No D5586 that an allocation was made elsewhere. Subsequently the class appeared in all parts of the old Eastern Region and, with the reduction of power requirements, became commonplace in former North Eastern Region territory and on the Western Region.

Internal troubles were however mounting. A series of crankcase fractures in the original Mirlees engines led eventually to the fitting of No D5677 of March with an English Electric 12SVT engine. Installed at Doncaster in 1964, it was an instant success. Similar to the engines in the Class 37, although not intercooled, it was arranged to deliver 1,470hp to suit the original electrical equipment, and as such operates at 400hp less than the full commercial rating. In the course of the ensuing couple of years, the entire class received the 12SVT engine during general overhauls; by 1969 the satisfactory level of 87% availability was being recorded.

Other modifications to the class have been the selective fitting of air brakes and the equipping of certain locomotives with electric train heating apparatus. These latter machines are classified as 31/4 instead of 31/1; the ETH facility is used in conjunction with empty stock working at major termini.

Right: No 31.019 storms through Brentwood on 28 September 1979 ready for the assault on Brentwood bank. This locomotive is maintained in a highly commendable external condition by Stratford, where it acquired a silver-grey roof and red buffer beams. *John Glover*

Left: Locomotive crews who are assigned to empty stock working know that much time is likely to be spent hanging around. The crew of No 31.222 catch up on the latest news in this night shot of Kings Cross on 16 December 1977. *Geoff Gillham*

Below: No 31.411 is one of the locomotives adorned with a waist level white stripe. It is seen here passing Wood Green with a down empty stock train on 26 July 1979. *Brian Morrison*

Right: There are no longer any through trains to Cambridge via the GN route. On 2 July 1977 an unidentified Class 31 crosses Welwyn viaduct with the 17.30 Kings Cross to Cambridge. *Stanley Creer*

Below right: The 09.15 (SO) Yarmouth to Manchester Piccadilly is seen near Two Mile Bottom behind 31.322 on 3 June 1978. *John Baker*

Above left: Near Saxham and Risby, No 31.208 is in charge of the 18.25 (SX) Ipswich to Whitemoor freight on 14 April 1978. *John Baker*

Left: Coal empties on another Ipswich-Whitemoor working crossing a drain near Manea headed by No 31.325 on 9 June 1975. *Stanley Creer*

Above: No 31.240 passes Kennet station with the 07.52 (SX) freight from Whitemoor to Bury St Edmunds on 9 May 1978. *John Baker*

Right: Entering Whitemoor yard from the south is No 31.164 on 12 July 1979. *Geoff Dowling*

Above left: Skegness station on 14 June 1975 with the 14.00 (SO) to Chesterfield waiting to depart behind No 31.224. The vast capacity of this Lincolnshire terminus is now sadly underused. *Stanley Creer*

Left: No 31.225 takes part in reballasting work at Copmanthorpe, near York, in June 1977. *Les Nixon*

Above: The 12.40 (SO) Blackpool North to Leeds has taken York based No 31.111 into London Midland Region territory. The train is approaching Diggle on 14 July 1979. *David Flitcroft*

Right: No 5539, now 31.121, is seen on empty stock duties at Paddington whilst Class 52 No 1040 *Western Queen* arrives with a train from South Wales on 25 April 1973. *Philip Hawkins*

Above: The 14.10 Exeter St Davids to Paignton leaves
Newton Abbot behind No 31.136 on 2 July 1979.
Brian Morrison

Above right: A Bristol Temple Meads to Portsmouth
Harbour train headed by No 31.243 approaches
Westbury on 16 September 1978. *John Vaughan*

Right: The 16.10 Bristol Temple Meads to Weymouth
has No 31.423 in charge as it passes Sydney Gardens,
Bath, on 14 March 1979. *Geoff Dowling*

Below: Nos 31.257 and 31.230 near Dorridge on the spring morning of 8 April 1976 with the 06.45 Paddington to Birmingham New Street.   *Philip Hawkins*

Bottom: The 14.45 Paddington to Birmingham New Street climbs Hatton bank in the charge of Nos 31.304 and 31.256 on 18 September 1976.   *Geoff Dowling*

Class 40:
English Electric Type 4

The English Electric Type 4 is a massive machine. In the initial stages of dieselisation, the civil engineers were particularly concerned about the effects the new-fangled diesels would have on their track, and following analysis of the causes of track stresses and failures in the United States the specifications were drawn up. These included the stipulation that the maximum axle-load permitted would be 20 tons (with 19 tons being desirable) and the axle-load to wheel diameter ratio should not exceed 4.5.

Within such parameters, the 1Co-Co1 wheel arrangement was a necessity for a Type 4 diesel-electric using a medium speed engine. Power was provided by the 16SVT Mk II engine, which develops 2,000hp at 850rev/min. This 16-cylinder V-form engine was no stranger to the BR scene, as its forerunners had been installed in the postwar LMS and SR main line diesels. Four Napier turbo-chargers are used to pressure charge the engine, and it is the distinctive sound of these at work which has given these locomotives the name of 'Whistlers'. Three nose-suspended traction motors are mounted on each bogie, one to each driving axle, and driving through single reduction spur gears.

Of the total weight of 133 tons, only 108 tons is available for adhesion through the driving wheels. The diameter of these is 3ft 9in, but that of the carrying wheels is only 3ft 0in. The high total weight at least had the advantage of ensuring good braking performance when working unfitted freight trains. Nevertheless, a length of 69ft 6in and a weight of 149lb for each horsepower developed compares unfavourably with more modern designs.

On 14 March 1958 No D200 was delivered from Newton-le-Willows to Doncaster BR works for acceptance trials. This was the first Type 4 diesel to be delivered under the pilot scheme, and in the following four years a total of 200 machines was completed. One hundred and eighty were erected at Vulcan Foundry, the remainder coming from the Robert Stephenson and Hawthorn works at Darlington. As built, locomotives to No D323 had the old style marker lights; Nos D324-D344 had the split headcode boxes one on each side of the communicating doors, and No D345 onwards had a centrally placed four character indicator. Various changes have since taken place; in particular many of the doors are now permanently sealed.

Five of the first 10 locomotives to be delivered were sent to the Great Eastern, where they exhibited 'exceptional powers of acceleration and hill climbing' compared with the 'Britannia' Pacifics on the Liverpool Street-Norwich runs. The first 27 of the 1959 build went to the London Midland Region, and all but two of these were given names associated with the shipping industry, because of their employment on Liverpool-London boat trains in pre-electrification days. Few, if any, of these names are still carried. The class allocations have always been to the London Midland, Eastern and Scottish Regions, and they are frequently to be seen all over the North of England. Lack of electric train heating equipment has limited their employment on Inter-City services in recent years, although many are dual brake fitted; consequently the greater part of their work is on freight. Many have now had their train heating boilers removed and are thus unable to heat passenger trains. In the early days a water scoop had been fitted so that the 800 gallon tank could be refilled from the still extant water troughs as an alternative to the water column!

Over the years the Class 40s have shown their worth, maintaining an availability of 80%. By 1966, the class had completed 100 million miles in service, the then highest total of any class in the BR diesel fleet. Despite admissions in 1961 that 2,000hp was insufficient power for the needs of the day, no development work was undertaken. Thoughts of applying inter-cooling to the engine, which might have raised its output to 2,400hp, never materialised.

Below: No 40.018 with its number painted on the connecting doors leaves Belmont Tunnel, Bangor, with the 12.57 Holyhead to Euston on 29 August 1979. This locomotive was previously named *Carmania*. *Larry Goddard*

Right: No 40.113 appears to have certain internal troubles as it passes Prestatyn at 70mph on 4 August 1979. The train is the 11.05 Manchester Victoria to Holyhead. *Larry Goddard.*

Below right: Passing Colwyn Bay with the 16.25 Holyhead to Euston on 3 September 1975 is No 40.045. *David Flitcroft*

Left: On 17 August 1978, No 40.094 negotiates the bridge at Frodsham with a Manchester-bound freight. *Les Nixon*

Below left: A Class 40 leaves Manchester Victoria with the 12.42 to Llandudno on 10 September 1977. To the right are the disused platforms of Manchester Exchange; the two stations together once boasted the longest platform in the British Isles. *David Flitcroft*

Above right: No 40.107 heads an up ballast train between Llandudno Junction and Colwyn Bay on 9 August 1977. *Wyn Hobson*

Centre right: Deputising for a failed dmu, No 40.055 is in charge of the 15.56 to Oldham. The train is leaving Manchester Victoria on 23 February 1979. *Geoff Dowling*

Below: No 40.132 nears Droylesden with a long welded rail train on Sunday 8 July 1979. *David Flitcroft*

Above: With Kearsley power station in the background, No 40.112 nears Kearsley station with a northbound freight on 15 November 1974.   *David Flitcroft*

Left: On 14 September 1978, No 40.134 passes Ulverston with a train for Barrow-in-Furness. *Chris Davis*

Above right: An animated scene at Skipton on Sunday 29 April 1979. No 40.019 (previously *Caronia*) draws away from its northbound freight, to be exchanged for No 40.143 in the foreground. Meanwhile, No 40.092 passes through with a southbound train.   *Chris Davis*

Right; On the Settle and Carlisle line, a Class 40 approaches Blea Moor with a block train of Presflos on 3 May 1975.   *Chris Davis*

Far right: Near Todmorden on the Calder Valley line, No 40.038 is in charge of the Heaton to Manchester Red Bank newspaper empties on 9 July 1978.   *Les Nixon*

Above left: No 40.003 passes Marsden at the eastern approach to Standedge Tunnel with a westbound grain train on 15 May 1979. *Geoff Dowling*

Left: At Earles' sidings, Hope, No 40.016 (previously *Campania*) is ready to leave. The rails are being sanded to give the locomotive better adhesion. The date is 1 December 1978. *Les Nixon*

Above: Also at Earles' sidings, No 40.119 on the right is waiting to return light engine to Manchester whilst No 40.100 passes with the Grimsby to Manchester empty newspaper vans on 18 February 1978. *Les Nixon*

Centre right: No 40.091 gets a clear road through Barrow Hill Junction with a northbound oil train on 26 January 1979. *Chris Davis*

Below right: No 40.196 passes Kennet with the 10.09 (SX) air-braked freight service from Whitemoor to Parkeston on 2 January 1979. *John Baker*

Top: No 40.029 (previously *Saxonia*) collects a 54-tonne payload VTG ferryvan and three loaded bulk grain vans from Banks' siding at Kennet to attach to the 11.45 freight from Bury St Edmunds to Whitemoor on 21 March 1979. The ferryvan had brought in binding compound to convert second class grain into cattle cake, and the bulk grain vans contain barley for Burton. *John Baker*

Above: The 08.30 Kings Cross to Cleethorpes leaves Market Rasen behind No 40.036 on 13 June 1975. *Stanley Creer*

Top right: Near North Queensferry, No 40.123 is in charge of an Inverness to Edinburgh express on 20 April 1979. *Les Nixon*

Right: In the evening of 2 April 1979, No 40.061 leaves Aberdeen with the 19.02 parcels to Perth. *Cyril Lofthus*

52

Class 504:
Manchester-Bury Electric Units

Unique amongst British Rail electrification systems, the former Lancashire and Yorkshire Railway's Manchester-Bury Bolton Street line is equipped with the 1,200V dc side contact system. Conversion to the standard ac overhead system has been considered more than once — first in the late 1950s before the present trains were ordered, and later as part of the abortive Picc-Vic Tunnel proposals. In 1959, the renewal of rolling stock became a necessity, whilst the lineside electrical equipment was in good repair. Consequently, the side contact system was perpetuated and 26 two-car units were constructed at Wolverton Works. Each set consists of a Driving Trailer Composite (since converted locally to Open Second class accommodation) and a Driving Motor Open Brake Second which is fitted with two English Electric 141hp traction motors.

Below: In days gone by, Bury had two stations; confusingly one travelled to Bolton from Knowsley Street, not Bolton Street! This is Bolton Street station, itself now abandoned in favour of a new location with bus-rail interchange. The 12.00 to Manchester Victoria departs on 4 April 1978. *Wyn Hobson*

Right: Heaton Park station was undergoing reconstruction on 10 June 1978 as the 17.20 from Bury entered the platform. *David Flitcroft*

Below right: The 12.00 Bury to Manchester Victoria approaches Radcliffe on 4 January 1979. *David Flitcroft*

Below, far right: Near Whitefield on 29 August 1978 is the 15.20 from Bury. *David Flitcroft*

Classes 83 and 86:
ac Electric Locomotives

English Electric was one of the five contractors who built ac electric locomotives for the inauguration of the London Midland Region electrification. Introduced in 1960, all the 25kV Bo-Bo machines were designed to a common specification. They were to be capable of hauling a 475 ton passenger train from Manchester to London at a maximum speed of 100mph with an average speed of 67mph, inclusive of one stop of one minute duration, and running for four miles at 15mph; they were also to be able to haul 950ton freights at an average 42mph. Axle-load was not to exceed 20 tons, and a flexible drive arrangement was specified to reduce the unsprung weight to a minimum. Cab layouts, controls and certain mechanical parts were also standardised, and so, initially, were mercury arc rectifiers. All were originally fitted with a pair of Stone Faiveley pantographs, although one was subsequently removed.

The 15 English Electric AL3 locomotives turned out to be the shortest at 52ft 6in and lightest at 76 tons of the five designs, with a continuous rating of 2,960hp. Four English Electric springborne dc traction motors of 740hp were fitted, with SLM resilient drives. At about £50,000 each, they were roundly one quarter of the cost of a 'Deltic'. One locomotive, No E3100, took part in a successful experiment with transducers, a means of giving stepless power control.

The mercury arc rectifiers gave repeated trouble, and with the delivery of the Class 86 locomotives the Class 83s were eventually stored as surplus to traffic requirements. Electrification to Glasgow required their return to traffic, and the locomotives were extensively rebuilt at Doncaster Works. This included the substitution of silicon rectifiers for the mercury arc type.

The purpose of ordering five designs totalling 100 locomotives was to derive a satisfactory standard for future production. 1965 saw the appearance of the first of the AL6 locomotives which were ordered in 1962. Several changes were made as a result of experience, the most important being the abandonment of flexible drives and the substitution of conventional axle-hung nose suspended traction motors. This was expected to save £3,000 per locomotive in capital costs and also to reduce maintenance. Other innovations were the fitting of only one pantograph, omission of the voltage changeover equipment (which had never been used on the originals anyway), and a general simplification. The reduction of wheel diameter from 4ft 0in to 3ft 9in allowed useful additional headroom in the body.

Of the 100 Class 86 locomotives, English Electric erected 60 at Vulcan Foundry, the remainder coming from BR Doncaster. The locomotives were very much a cooperative effort between the railway and private industry; English Electric supplied all rectifiers, transformers and control gear, wheelslip protection and some of the auxiliary machines. Most of the remaining components came from AEI, including the crossed-arm pantographs fitted to 10 locomotives, but all the bogies were constructed at Doncaster. The class each weigh 81 tons and most have a continuous rating of 3,600hp; the final 40 are uprated to 4,040hp for working heavier trains or, alternatively, climbing more severe grades at lower speeds and achieving a higher tractive effort without overheating.

Unfortunately, the decision not to use flexible drives was ill-judged. The high unsprung weight of the traction motors played havoc with the track, and due to body pitching the riding qualities of the locomotives deteriorated. The axle loading was nearly four tons in excess of that of the 'Deltics'. No E3173 was chosen for experiment, and emerged in 1969 fitted with prominent helical springs. It was unofficially named *Zebedee,*

Below: No 83.001 is captured for the camera at Longsight depot on 28 April 1979. *Les Nixon*

and after exhaustive tests it was followed in 1972 by the conversion of a further 57 locomotives fitted with resilient wheels and flexicoil suspension; these are designated Class 86/2. Three more locomotives classified 86/1 are fitted with Class 87 type locomotive bogies. The remaining unconverted locomotives became Class 86/0 and are officially limited to 80mph and restricted to freight haulage; some have been fitted with jumper cables for working in multiple. However, in a further modification, Sab resilient wheels are being fitted to restore the 100mph capability. Locomotives so treated are reclassified 86/3, and are being renumbered accordingly.

Above: Leaving Primrose Hill Tunnel on 6 June 1973 is No 83.012 with an up express. *Brian Morrison*

Centre left: No 83.012 again, this time in the Lune Valley alongside the M6 with an up Motorail train on 3 June 1977. *Brian Morrison*

Below left: No 83.015 approaches Penrith with a down parcels in July 1977. *Peter Robinson*

Above right: No 86.001 passes through Holmes Chapel with a Manchester bound parcels train on 15 August 1979. Parcels vans are some of the oldest rolling stock in use today; the first two vehicles are ex-LMS vans built to a design originating in the 1920s. *Larry Goddard*

Right: At Crawford on 19 April 1979, No 86.039 heads south with a Glasgow to Euston express. *Les Nixon*

Above left: The 12.00 Euston to Carlisle hurries through Tebay behind No 86.036 on 12 June 1974. *Brian Morrison*

Centre left: No 86.033 is seen passing South Hampstead with northbound empty stock on 9 June 1979. *Wyn Hobson*

Below left: One of the only three locomotives of Class 86/1, No 86.101 *Sir William A. Stanier FRS* leaves Crewe with the 08.30 Manchester Piccadilly to Swansea on 17 March 1979. *David Flitcroft*

Above: No 86.254 displays its Flexicoil suspension as it passes Lichfield Trent Valley No 1 box with the 07.05 Glasgow Central to Euston on 30 August 1978. *Geoff Dowling*

Right: In the days when certain Manchester-London trains ran via Birmingham, No 86.242 hauls the 16.23 Manchester Piccadilly to Euston near Hampton-in-Arden on 14 May 1974. *Philip Hawkins*

Above: The late evening sun catches No 86.256 running into Stoke-on-Trent with the 1912 Manchester Piccadilly to Euston on 7 June 1979.   *Kevin Lane*

Right: No 86.241 now *Glenfiddich,* passes Etruia with the 13.55 Euston to Manchester Piccadilly on 1 June 1976. *Les Nixon*

Classes 302, 306 and 308:

Eastern's Electric Units

For the 1949 Shenfield electrification, 92 three-car 1,500V dc units were provided, and each was equipped with four English Electric 210hp traction motors. Come the 1960 changeover to 25kV/6.25kV ac operation, the units had to be converted, and this was achieved by installing the transforming and rectifying equipment in the vehicle adjacent to the power car. Rectified ac was thus fed to the original dc motors; the conversion was carried out at Stratford, using AEI equipment. Faiveley pantographs, together with air blast circuit breakers, were fitted and the units classified 306.

1960 also saw the electrification of virtually all the Great Eastern suburban area and the London, Tilbury and Southend (LTS) line. A large quantity of new multiple units was required, and they were built in the railway workshops at York and Doncaster. English Electric supplied the power equipment for 157 of the (mainly) four-car units. All followed the standard ac practice of concentrating the traction motors in one of the intermediate vehicles.

All the Eastern Region units were required to attain the same performance level. Within a maximum speed of 75mph, they had to be capable of running the 41.5 miles from Liverpool Street to Southend Victoria fully loaded in 60 minutes with six intermediate stops of 30 seconds each. An acceleration rate from stand of 1.1mph per second was specified, and, no doubt with Brentwood bank in mind, they had to be able to re-start on a 1 in 70 gradient with two traction motors cut out.

The principal English Electric contract concerned the LTS sets numbered 201-312, ordered in 1957. Delivered from November 1958, these were the first 25kV 50Hz units in the United Kingdom. Four 192hp traction motors were fitted, together with excitron rectifiers. The final unit, No 312, was for a time the subject of experiment with mercury-arc rectifiers and thyristors. Officially classified AM2 and then Class 302, the LTS units seat 19 first class and 344 second class passengers. They are deemed to be capable of carrying the same number again as a standing load. Despite early troubles with insulation faults in the traction motors, these trains have given good service, although the excitron rectifiers were abandoned in favour of silicon in subsequent orders.

Nine more units, Nos 313-321, were built in 1961 for the LTS services, and these incorporated a non-driving motor luggage van. Units Nos 313-6 had this vehicle converted to passenger accommodation in 1971 and are classified 308/4; those retaining their original configuration form Class 308/2.

To supplement the 32 former dc units dating from 1956 and used on the Southend Victoria services, a further 33 'GE outer suburban' units were ordered and these appeared in 1961. Numbered 133-165 they incorporate four 200hp traction motors and are classified 308/1. The remaining English Electric equipments are fitted to the final three Enfield and Chingford units numbered 453-5 of Class 308/3.

Above left: Class 306 'Shenfield' unit No 050 leads a nine-car formation over the Ilford flyover and into Ilford station on 28 September 1979. *John Glover*

Centre left: At Gidea Park, passengers change from the inner suburban services to the Southend line trains. Class 308/1 unit No 149 arrives with the 15.12 from Liverpool Street on the same day. *John Glover*

Below: Class 308/1 unit No 163 is at the front of the 11.45 for Liverpool Street as it leaves Southend Victoria on 12 September 1976. *Brian Morrison*

Right: Class 302 unit No 268 runs into Fenchurch Street with all doors opening (and showing Liverpool Street on the blind!) on 30 October 1979. *Peter Shoesmith*

Below right: Ascending Brentwood bank is Class 302 unit No 202 with the 09.34 Liverpool Street to Southend Victoria on 19 May 1977. *Brian Morrison*

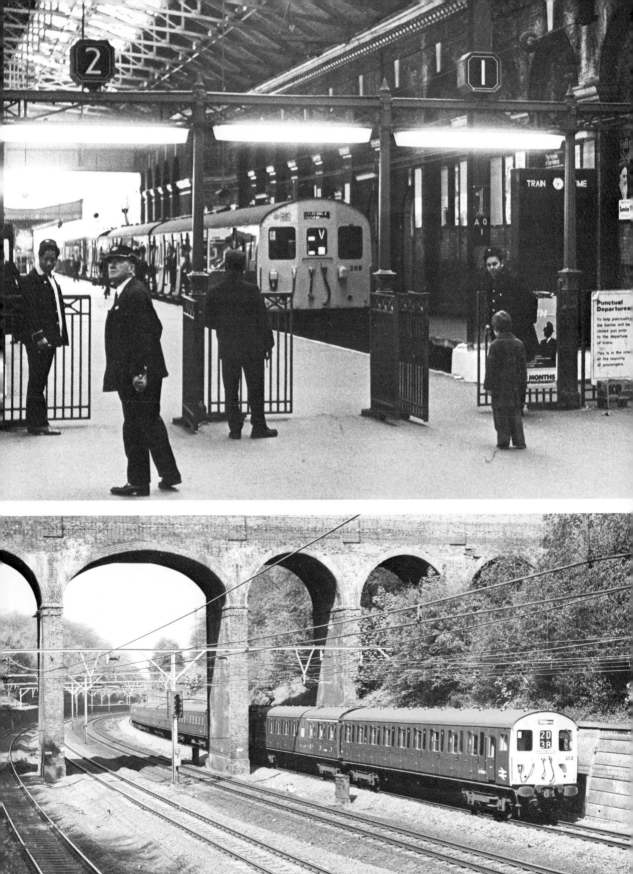

Above left: Approaching Dagenham Dock on 9 February 1978 is Class 302 unit No 263 with the 11.57 Leigh-on-Sea to Fenchurch Street.   *John Glover*

Left: Class 302 unit No 225 arrives at Purfleet on 26 September 1979 with a Shoeburyness to Fenchurch Street via Tilbury service.   *John Glover*

Above: Class 308/2 unit No 320 passes Grays on a wet morning. The date is 1 March 1977. Second vehicle from the front is the motor luggage van, which on the Class 308/4 units has been converted to passenger accommodation.   *John Glover*

Right: Only three trains of the 'Enfield and Chingford' units are equipped with English Electric traction motors. Class 308/3 unit No 453 prepares to leave the single-tracked Ware station for Hertford East in September 1974.   *John Glover*

Class 37:
English Electric Type 3

December 1960 saw the delivery of the first of what was to become known as the Class 37 locomotive, a design which was eventually to run to 309 units. No D6700 was erected at Vulcan Foundry which was responsible for 242 of the class, the remainder coming from Robert Stephenson and Hawthorn. The engine installed is the 12CSVT, a 12-cylinder inter-cooled version of the V-16 type used in the Class 40; it provides 1,750hp at 850rev/min. Intercooling is a means of reducing the temperature of the pressure charged air from the supercharger before it enters the engine. To do this, the air is passed over tubes through which cooling water is pumped. Six axle-hung nose-suspended traction motors with single reduction spur gearing are fitted; these are identical and indeed interchangeable with those fitted to the 'Deltics'. Despite its construction as a Co-Co, the Class 37 is still a weighty machine, and its 105 tons total weight equates to an axle-load of 17.5tons. It can negotiate a curve down to four chains radius.

The first 119 locomotives were equipped with route indicator boxes either side of the nose end doors, some of which have been subsequently sealed up. From No D6819 onwards, the doors were dispensed with, and the four-character indicator was mounted centrally. Some criticism was directed at the locomotive's appearance. Comments ranged from 'far from graceful' to 'an elephant of a locomotive'.

A maximum speed of 90mph makes the class suitable for passenger work, although it is only on the Great Eastern where they are regularly thus employed in any quantity.

Passenger train haulage requires an ability to provide train heating, and some are fitted with a Clayton boiler. As built, the class were fitted with a fuel tank of 830 gallons capacity, an auxiliary 120gallon tank, and a water tank for the train heating boiler which held 800 gallons. Some Western Region locomotives have had the water tank converted to a fuel tank at Cardiff Canton, raising the total fuel capacity to 1,750 gallons. Another class variation is the fitting of dual braking in certain cases.

The delivery of No D6988 to the WR in 1965 marked the 2,000th diesel engine supplied to British Rail by English Electric; at that time the cost of each locomotive was quoted as £83,250. Two years later, the class was achieving the highest availability and lowest casualty rate of any of British Rail's diesel fleet. This was due in part no doubt to the conservative rating of the 12CSVT engine; notwithstanding examples of its being uprated elsewhere, and notably to 2,025hp in East Africa, no attempt has been made to increase its performance at home.

Apart from a handful based in Scotland, the Class 37s are split on a roughly 2:1 ratio between the Eastern Region and South Wales depots of the Western Region.

Right: There are a few workings from Yarmouth to London via Cambridge. No 37.035 passes Padnal with the 09.35 (SO) from Yarmouth to Liverpool Street on 28 July 1979. *John Baker*

Above right inset: No 37.033 departs from platform 10 at Liverpool Street with a Harwich Boat Train on 27 May 1978. *John Howie*

Left: The 08.25 (SO) Newcastle to Yarmouth nears Two Mile Bottom behind No 37.089 on 3 June 1978. *John Baker*

Below left: No 37.173 enters Thetford with the 09.56 (SX) freight from Whitemoor to Norwich on 5 March 1979. *John Baker*

Right: No 37.095 is seen at Sleaford on 19 August 1978 with a Saturdays only train from Skegness. *Les Nixon*

Below: A Working Men's Club excursion to Scarborough leaves Barnsley behind No 37.095 on 9 July 1978. *Les Nixon*

Above left: No 37.053 passes Oakenshaw North Junction signalbox with an up oil train on 16 July 1979. *Les Nixon*

Centre left: Nos 37.166 and 37.070 skirt the coast at Brotton with an ICI potash train from Boulby on 24 August 1978. *Les Nixon*

Below left: Nos 37.032 and 37.197 take the Newcastle line out of Carlisle and are photographed to the east of Petteril Bridge Junction on 21 August 1979. *Terry Flinders*

Right: A Sunderland bound coal train passes Newcastle Central on 25 September 1976 behind Nos 37.194 and 37.249. *Philip Hawkins*

Below: Beside the sea at Burnmouth, No 37.161 heads an up oil train on 30 May 1977. *Les Nixon*

Top: In the early morning mist at Pilning on 24 April 1975, No 37.308 is in charge of an eastbound freight. *Philip Hawkins*

Above: No 37.281 (on left) meets No 37.279 at Radyr on typical South Wales coal workings on 30 August 1978. This area is one of the last in South Wales to retain semaphore signals. *Geoff Gillham*

74

Above: With its number unofficially painted in red above the bufferbeam, No 37.288 rejoins the main line at Taffs Well with a train of empties from Nantgarw Coke Ovens on the same day. *Geoff Gillham*

Below: The 'Western Requiem' excursion from Paddington to the Welsh valleys is seen passing Dinas Rhondda on the Treherbert to Pontypridd leg of the run behind No 37.189 on 20 February 1977. *Les Nixon*

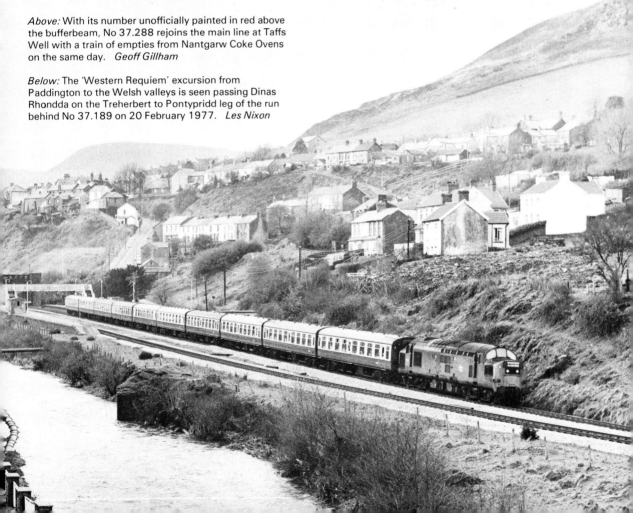

Above: The 16.18 Swansea to Milford Haven approaches Llandore in the charge of No 37.182 on 25 August 1979. *Les Nixon*

Right: A train of empty wagons trundles through Hither Green with No 37.060 in charge on 21 October 1978. *David Flitcroft*

Class 55:
'Deltics'

One of the undoubted highlights of the dieselisation of British Rail was the delivery from English Electric of the fleet of 'Deltics' in 1961-2. Developed from the 1955 prototype which, interestingly, was designed for passenger or freight work, the 22 production models were not part of the Modernisation Plan. This had envisaged the East Coast and West Coast main lines being electrified concurrently, but it soon became clear that this was a practical impossibility. The 'Deltics' were therefore seen as a stop-gap replacement for steam until such time as electrification could be completed.

Based on a pair of Napier Deltic D18-25 18-cylinder units, each rated at 1,650hp at 1,500rev/min, the three banks of cylinders are arranged in the form of an equilateral triangle. The cost of the locomotives, reported to be around £200,000 each, was considered to be exceptional at the time — but this was an exceptional locomotive. It was the first on British Rail to exceed the 2,000/2,500hp barrier, and it did so by a substantial margin. It was also capable of 105mph. The Deltic engine itself was the key, being powerful in relation to its weight and size. Through keeping the total weight down to 99 tons, an axle-load of only 16.5 tons resulted, and this with a Co-Co design and a length equal to the Class 40. It was thus possible to avoid the 1Co-Co1 arrangement of the Type 4 designs and still keep within the civil engineer's requirements.

A novel maintenance agreement was concluded with the manufacturers with payment subject to the locomotives attaining a guaranteed contract mileage in service. In practice it proved impossible to diagram the locomotives to achieve the specified 220,000 annual mileage per machine, and the scheme actually operated on the fulfilment of the diagrammed mileage. Nevertheless, the results were spectacular. In the first $5\frac{1}{2}$ years of operation, the fleet covered 21 million miles — the equivalent of 500 miles for each locomotive every day. In under 12 years from its delivery from Vulcan Foundry, No D9010 *The King's Own Scottish Borderer* of Haymarket clocked up two million miles. The initial maintenance agreements expired from 1966 onwards, whereupon British Rail took over the maintenance itself. Retention of 12 English Electric engineers at the three motive power depots (Finsbury Park, Gateshead and Haymarket) and at Doncaster was felt to be unnecessarily costly. Until 1971 however, engine overhauls were still carried out by the manufacturers.

The fine performances put up by the 'Deltic' fleet on the East Coast main line are legion, but such had been the growth of traffic by the 1970s that the 'Deltics' were rostered for less than half the daytime Inter-City expresses from Kings Cross. Even 3,300hp had its limitations in respect of commercial needs, and the limited 'Deltic + 8' (coach) trains of 280 tons became well known to business travellers between London, the North East and West Yorkshire. Despite their success, the 'Deltics' were not considered as one of the standard types of BR diesels, and the fleet was never expanded.

All members of the class are named; those originally allocated to Finsbury Park recall famous racehorses, whilst the others carry regimental names.

Due to their pre-eminence in the express passenger fleet, 'Deltics' were fitted with electric train heating apparatus at an early stage in the changeover programme. No D9007 *Pinza* was the first to be equipped in 1967; all of the class are of course dual braked. A minor 'first' for the class was the selection of *Alycidon*, by now No 55.009, to be fitted with the now familiar twin marker lights which replaced the four-character headcodes; this modification was carried out in 1972.

Right: No 55.007 *Pinza* with white painted window surrounds passes New Barnet with the 12.05 Kings Cross to Hull on 27 August 1979. *Wyn Hobson*

Far right: On the same day, No 55.014 *The Duke of Wellington's Regiment* crosses Welwyn Viaduct with the 16.05 Kings Cross to York. *Wyn Hobson*

Below right: Sunday permanent way work may bring luckless passengers a diversion via Cambridge. On 7 November 1976, a 'Deltic' passes Shepreth Branch Junction box with the 13.00 Kings Cross to Edinburgh. *Les Nixon*

Below: The inaugural 'Silver Jubilee' leaves Copenhagen Tunnel on 8 June 1977 behind suitably turned out 'Deltic' No 55.012 *Crepello*. *Brian Morrison*

Bottom right: The open-ness of the East Coast main line is apparent in this view of No 55.015 *Tulyar* at Woodcroft Crossing with the 12.50 Leeds to Kings Cross on 4 November 1978. *John Baker*

Above left: An atmospheric shot of a 'Deltic' at Bathley Lane on 16 April 1979. *John East*

Above: On the same day, another 'Deltic' passes South Muskham, near Newark. *John East*

Left: No 9002 (now 55.002) *The King's Own Yorkshire Light Infantry* runs non-stop through Doncaster on the rainy 21 September 1972. The train is the 14.00 Kings Cross to Edinburgh. *Terry Flinders*

Above: No 55.021 *Argyll and Sutherland Highlander* brings the up 'Hull Executive' into Doncaster at 08.05 on 22 August 1979. *Terry Flinders*

Left: Holgate Junction, York sees No 55.020 *Nimbus* accelerating away with the 12.40 Edinburgh to Kings Cross on 23 September 1976. *Philip Hawkins*

Top: No 55.019 *Royal Highland Fusilier* enters York on 24 January 1976 with the 08.00 Kings Cross to Edinburgh. *Geoff Dowling*

Above: With the Minster just visible over the station canopy, No 55.013 *The Black Watch* hauls the 10.50 Kings Cross to Newcastle out of York on 31 August 1978. *David Flitcroft*

Top right: The traditional view of York station. No 55.016 *Gordon Highlander* stands in platform 9 on 11 August 1976 with the 07.45 Kings Cross to Edinburgh. *Geoff Dowling*

Right: Crossing the Royal Border Bridge, Berwick is No 55.003 *Meld* on 16 July 1976 with the same train. *Geoff Dowling*

Above: No 55.015 *Tulyar* passes Grantshouse on
21 May 1977 with an Edinburgh to Kings Cross train.
Cyril Lofthus

Right: 'Deltics' are rarely seen outside the Eastern and
Scottish Regions. No 55.003 *Meld* heads an up special
through South Marston cutting east of Swindon on
12 October 1975.   *Terry Flinders*

Below: The 16.00 to Kings Cross leaves Edinburgh
behind No 55.011 *The Royal Northumberland Fusiliers*
on 26 April 1975.   *Cyril Lofthus*

Class 73:
Electro-Diesels

Although first mooted in the early postwar years, it was not until 1962 that the first electro-diesels appeared. In a largely electrified system, it was foreseen that the electro-diesel would be capable of freight work in non-electrified sidings with safety for those on the ground and without the cost of electrification. It would also have its uses in dock locations where third-rail supply was impracticable, and during track possessions by the civil engineer when the current was switched off. Other uses also arise in non-electrified areas, but on the whole only limited diesel power was needed. By 1956 the concept was of a 'Heavy Motor Luggage Van' utilising a Hastings diesel electric power unit with luggage space and an additional driving position. However, doubts as to its operational utility led to the present design at the time of ordering in 1959.

Universal availability and the maximum standardisation led to a body constructed to the Hastings loading gauge and use of the 4SRKT MkII engine of 600hp. Four English Electric 400hp nose suspended traction motors are provided, driving through spur gears and giving up to 1,600hp in the electric mode. In general terms it is the equal of a Class 33 when working as an electric, and on test accelerated a 700ton train up a 1 in 250 gradient to 30mph in four minutes.

Whilst the first six (Class 73/0) were erected at Eastleigh, the second order went to English Electric for 43 complete locomotives (Class 73/1). Changes were made to the auxiliary power supply system to make it compatible with that used in electric units, but the latter locomotives can only provide train heating when working as electrics.

With a diesel engine in No 1 end of the locomotive, some counterbalance was required. The buffer beam at No 2 end was thus deliberately made thicker and heavier to provide a better distribution of the 75 tons total weight. Drivers are instructed to run the diesel engine once per shift. The change in power supply can be achieved at any time without bringing the locomotive to a stand; the pick up shoes are automatically retracted when the changeover is made. Maximum permitted speed is 80mph for the 73/0 version (classified JA by the Southern) and 90mph for the later JB locomotives introduced in 1965. Perhaps it was inevitable that the enthusiast fraternity should corrupt Electro-Diesel to 'Edwards'.

In the headcode panel, provision was made for white markers to be displayed under the main indicators. These signified to signalmen that the locomotive could be routed off the third-rail, but this facility is no longer in use.

The electro-diesels have been remarkably free from serious problems and are well liked by train crews. Fears about the complications resulting from two master controllers and so on have proved groundless. In fact, series production produced a class of locomotive costing well below the straight diesel equivalent, and it is doubtful if the straight electric Class 71 locomotives would have ever been built had the electro-diesels appeared earlier on the scene.

Left: One of the six Eastleigh-built Class 73s, No 73.001 is seen near Deepcut with an up parcels train on 10 September 1979. *John Glover*

Above: No 73.119 passes East Croydon with a northbound train of engineering department wagons on 1 March 1979. *Kevin Lane*

Below left: 4 June was Derby Day 1979; No 73.142 hauls the Royal Train from Victoria to Tattenham Corner past Wandsworth Common. *Stanley Creer*

Below: Channel Islands Boat Trains are now in the hands of the Class 73s. No 73.127 is seen in Clapham Cutting with the morning train to Weymouth Quay on 11 April 1978. *John Glover*

Above: An unidentified Class 73 crosses the River Thames at Battersea on the West London Extension line with a train of vans from Hoo Junction to Acton. *Stanley Creer*

Left: A wet day in Clapham station yard. No 73.134 is shunting on 20 April 1978. *Geoff Dowling*

Right: No 73.130 was running light engine towards Kensington Olympia on 4 August 1978. The cabling in the extreme foreground is for the London Transport branch from Earls Court, which comes to the surface here. *John Glover*

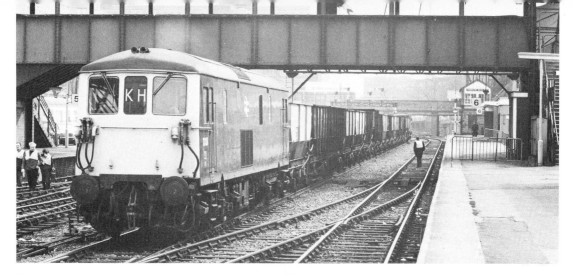

Top: The 24 March 1976 saw No 73.136 with a train of hopper wagons from Wimbledon to Acton at Kensington Olympia. *Brian Morrison*

Above: No 73.110 heads the up evening parcels service from Margate through Faversham on 30 June 1976. *Wyn Hobson*

Right: No 73.110 in company with No 73.115 approach Acton Wells Junction at no more than walking pace with a London Midland Region bound merry-go-round coal train on 26 July 1979. *Kevin Lane*

Class 310:
London Midland's
ac Electric Units

The arrival of the first of the 50 AM10 (Class 310) units for the London Midland Region in February 1965 heralded a considerable advance on earlier multiple-units. Designed at Doncaster, they were built at Derby and incorporated four English Electric 270hp traction motors of a similar design to that used in the Southern Region's 4REP Bournemouth express stock.

Novelties included integral stressed skin construction for the body to assist in load carrying. One result was that all power equipment has been underfloor mounted, and can be simply removed by fork lift truck. All equipment is either naturally cooled or self-ventilated; the traction motors draw filtered air through ducts in the coach side. Another innovation was the fitting of disc brakes. Besides reducing maintenance to a basic 14-day frequency, disc brakes eliminate the brake block dust which disfigures so many stations.

These units were the first to be delivered in the then new Rail Blue livery. They are only partially gangwayed in that there is no connection between the second and third vehicle in each set, although all passengers have access to toilet facilities. Riding qualities of these trains (maximum speed 75mph) have been compared with the best in Europe, and in 1970 the design was described as one of the most successful on British Rail.

Although provision was made for dual voltage equipment to be fitted, this has not proved necessary, and the Class 310 trains remain 25kV only. Some of the later units of Class 312 for the Great Eastern line are dual voltage, but these were supplied under GEC Traction auspices.

Below: With a crane from Willesden Freightliner Terminal just discernible in the background of this panned photograph, a Class 310 unit forms an evening northbound commuter service from Euston on 3 October 1977. *John Glover*

Left: Class 310 unit No 068 enters Rugby on 21 April 1979 with the 12.20 Birmingham New Street to Euston stopping service. *Brian Morrison*

Below left: Marston Green station attracts a substantial off-peak patronage. Class 310 unit No 082 calls with a Birmingham New Street to Euston train on 6 October 1979. *John Glover*

Above: Beside the Grand Union Canal to the north of Leighton Buzzard, a pair of Class 310 units form a Euston to Birmingham New Street stopping service in May 1977. *Kevin Lane*

Below: The local service up the Trent Valley is now very limited. At Nuneaton, Class 310 unit No 077 forms the 17.28 all stations to Stafford on 29 October 1976. *Peter Shoesmith*

Class 50:
Advanced Type 4

The Class 50 locomotives were designed by English Electric to British Rail specifications, and were the last new design to emerge before the GEC/AEI merger. In them was incorporated the logical development of the 16-cylinder engine employed in the Class 40s — the intercooled 16CSVT. It was arranged to deliver 2,700hp at 850rev/min.

Descended from the DP2 prototype, the locomotives contained some additional and advanced technology, with automatic tractive effort control, dynamic braking, inertia filtration and slow-speed control all fitted as standard. Although DP2 had been cheaper and lighter than the 'standard' Class 47, the production Class 50s turned out to be dearer, heavier and longer — largely because BR insisted on so many frills. Other features were more familiar, and the bogies and traction motors are similar to those installed in both the Class 37 and 55. Electric train heating was fitted from the outset.

The power/weight ratio of these machines at 23.5hp output per ton was a considerable improvement on the 15.0hp per ton of the Class 40, but still came nowhere near the phenomenal 33.3hp per ton of the 'Deltics'. English Electric guaranteed an 84% availability for the locomotives, with a penalty payable if a locomotive was stopped by either party. Unhappily, the trouble-free operation of DP2 was not mirrored in the Class 50s. A major failure of the little ends and the splitting of the cylinder liners led to two engines being written off, and this meant that only 48 engines were available for 50 locomotives. Use of the identical engine recovered from DP2 means that there is still one engine fewer than there are locomotives.

Originally the Class 50s were on hire to British Rail and carried a plate to that effect.

Leasing enables the customer to avoid the tying up of capital and thus spreads the cost over the life of the assets. In effect British Rail entered into a hire purchase agreement with English Electric, and in due course were able to purchase the locomotives for a nominal sum.

The class originally found employment north of Crewe. Although Nos D400/1 were fitted with jumper cables for working in multiple from new, subsequent class members carried only the necessary wiring. Crewe Works fitted jumpers to the remainder in anticipation of the 1970/1 accelerated West Coast timetable for which double heading was required. Following electrification, the class was transferred to the Western Region where its members are giving good service.

No D400 appeared in 1967, painted in Rail Blue with full yellow ends at the outset; the naming of these locomotives after 10 years operation caused minor variations to the livery and the placing of British Rail logo; they were never painted green. Those who had expected the locomotives to resemble the prototype were disappointed; initial thoughts on the appearance of the locomotives had to be modified due to British Rail requirements for a flat-fronted design and details of the cab layout.

The life of main line diesel locomotives was intended to be 25 years, but in the economic climate of the 1980s replacement of a large proportion of the fleet is out of the question. Consequently, action is being taken to refurbish certain locomotive classes, including the Class 50s, in an attempt to improve their reliability. Even so, a second series of heavy general repairs will be necessary to extend their life to 30 years; after this the locomotives will be worn out.

94

Above: Class 50s are no longer common-place on the London Midland Region. They have never been seen regularly in areas such as Melton Mowbray, which Nos 50.048 *Dauntless* and 50.010 *Monarch* are passing with a RPPR special on 18 March 1978. *Chris Davis*

Left: Flashback to 1970, and a Class 50 with a train of sheeted steel coil rumbles past Dentonholme Junction, Carlisle. *Peter Robinson*

95

Above: A Birmingham bound express passes Culham behind No 50.006 *Neptune* on 6 October 1979. *Les Nixon*

Centre left: No 50.026, now *Indomitable,* backs on to the 10.23 Manchester Piccadilly to Plymouth at Birmingham New Street on 18 March 1978. *Wyn Hobson*

Below left: Just before Christmas 1978, No 50.032 *Courageous* waits to depart from Paddington with the down 'Golden Hind'. *John Vaughan*

Above right: No 50.002 *Superb* heads the 06.15 Penzance to Paddington between Crofton and Savernake on 27 May 1978. In the foreground is the Kennet and Avon Canal. *John Vaughan*

Right: No 50.048 *Dauntless* is in charge of the down 'Cornish Riviera' on Good Friday 24 March 1978, and is seen here on the climb to Savernake summit. *John Vaughan*

Above: At Hungerford Crossing No 50.037, now *Illustrious,* passes with the 09.30 Paddington to Penzance on 28 December 1976. *Terry Flinders*

Centre left: The 07.53 Paignton to Paddington runs through Bedwyn at speed on 12 November 1974 behind No 50.003, now *Temeraire.* *Terry Flinders*

Below left: On Sundays in recent years, the line between Reading and Westbury has been closed due to engineering work and most West of England trains have been diverted via Bristol. Trains serving Westbury have to travel via Chippenham, Melksham and Trowbridge. On 16 July 1978 No 50.043 *Eagle* takes the Trowbridge line out of Westbury with the 15.15 from Paddington. *Geoff Gillham*

Right: West of Shrivenham
No 50.020, now *Revenge,* heads
the 15.23 Paddington to Bristol
Temple Meads on 7 May 1976.
Terry Flinders

Below: The 07.40 Paddington to
Bristol Temple Meads has mail
unloaded from the leading Brake
Second at Chippenham on
3 August 1976. The locomotive
is No 50.025, now *Invincible.*
Terry Flinders

Below right: No 50.038, now
Formidable, leaves Bristol Temple
Meads with the 11.47 Weston-
super-Mare to Paddington on
3 June 1976.   *Geoff Dowling*

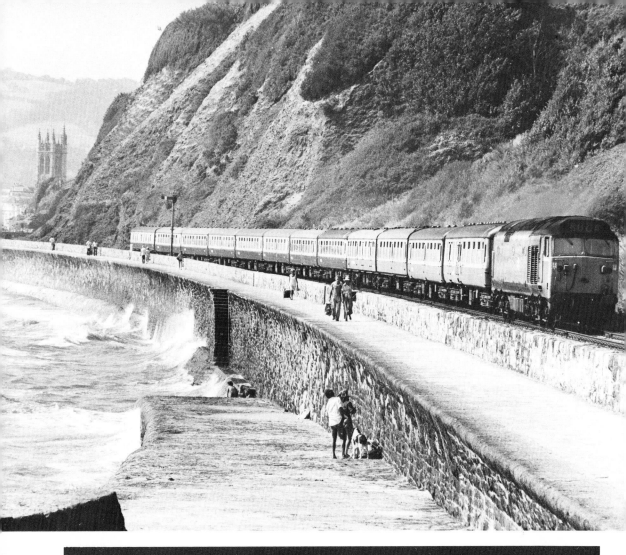

Left: Alongside the seawall at Teignmouth No 50.024, now *Vanguard*, is in charge of the 08.35 Penzance to Paddington. The date is 21 August 1976. *Geoff Dowling*

Below left: Between Dawlish and Teignmouth on 6 July 1979, No 50.047 *Swiftsure* heads an up engineer's stone train. *Brian Morrison*

Above: The railway runs close to the east side of the Teign estuary. No 50.030, now *Repulse*, is seen at Shaldon Bridge with the 07.55 Penzance to Liverpool Lime Street on 17 June 1975. *Terry Flinders*

Centre right: Descending Dainton bank on 2 July 1979 is No 50.011 *Centurion* with the 15.15 Plymouth to Manchester Piccadilly. *Brian Morrison*

Below right: An unidentified Class 50 crosses the Moorswater Viaduct with the up 'Cornish Riviera' on 26 March 1979. The piers of the original viaduct can be seen, as can the line to the china clay works. *John Glover*

Top: A critical inspection is afforded No 50.036 *Victorious* as it pauses at Bodmin Road with the 13.30 Paddington to Penzance on 16 June 1978. *John Vaughan*

Above: The 10.05 (FO) Penzance to Sheffield passes the remains of the tin-mining industry at Scorrier, near Redruth, behind No 50.002, now *Superb,* on 15 July 1977. *Brian Morrison*

Classes 405–430 and 487:
Southern's Electric Units

Throughout the period covered by this book, all power equipments for the Southern's fleet of electric multiple-units were supplied by English Electric until the end of that company's separate existence. The subject of a 10 year agreement between the railway and English Electric in 1936, the contract was renewed in 1946 and again in 1956. By 1965, over 2,000 equipments had been supplied, and the firm was able to claim that an English Electric powered train left one of the Southern's London termini every 15 seconds during peak hours. It is perhaps not necessary to stress the magnitude of the Southern's operations, but some figures released in respect of 1962 underlined its scale. In that year 292 million car miles (45 million train miles) were operated, during which time there were 1,690 on-line failures — equal to one failure per 173,000 car miles. This result was not considered particularly good, but the cost of maintenance — then at 1.2p per car mile — was set at the lowest possible level consistent with a reasonably acceptable failure rate. It says much for the soundness and simplicity of the designs that so little attention was required; one of the contributory reasons in later years may well have been the principle adhered to that the engineer responsible for design is also responsible for maintenance!

The standard equipment for Southern multiple-units has long been a pair of 250hp traction motors, axle mounted on the bogies of one vehicle of a two-car unit or on each of the end vehicles of four-car unit. However, the delivery from 1964 of the 4CIG units (Class 421), initially for the Brighton line, saw a change to the ac practice in which all power equipment is concentrated in one non-driving car for economy in maintenance. The Motor Saloon Brake Seconds in these trains thus contain four 250hp traction motors. The subsequent 4VEP (Class 423) units were similarly equipped, but the 4REP (Class 430) units for the Bournemouth electrification dating from 1967 required more power because of their specialised duties, and each of the two Driving

Right: Most venerable of the main Southern Region fleet of electric multiple-units are the 4SUBs, built in the early postwar years. Class 405/2 No 4641 calls at Ewell West with a Dorking to Waterloo commuter service on 11 April 1978. *John Glover*

Motor Saloon Seconds contains four 348hp traction motors. The four car unit therefore provides no less than 2,784hp, but this is of course required to power a 12-car train of 437 tons.

Further non-standard units are the Class 419 Motor Luggage Vans which are equipped with traction batteries for working on non-electrified lines — principally at the Channel Ports. They are also fitted with two 250hp motors, and as a result can haul a trailing load of up to 100 tons. Normally they work in multiple on Boat Trains.

Lastly, the Waterloo and City Line trains were built complete by English Electric in 1938. These Class 487 trains consist of 12 Motor Open Brake Seconds with 40 seats and 16 Trailer Open Seconds with 52 seats. These diminutive vehicles are only 47ft 0in long and 8ft 7.75in wide; their height is 9ft 7in 'with pantograph folded' according to some English Electric sales literature! Maximum speed is 40mph on the five minute journey between the two stations. Motor coaches are fitted with two 190hp totally enclosed traction motors and weigh 28 tons; the trailers weigh 19 tons. The normal formation is two motor cars sandwiching three trailers, an assembly which provides 236 seats. Officially, there is space for a further 360 standing.

Left: Class 405/2 No 4601 approaches Coulsdon North in 1975 with a Central Division suburban service. The line on the left is the Tattenham Corner branch which, although adjacent to the main line at this point, has no physical connection nearer than Purley, 1.5 miles further north. *Michael Baker*

Bottom left: EPB units form the mainstay of Tattenham Corner workings. Class 416/1 No 5652 runs into Tadworth with a London bound train in July 1976. *John Glover*

Right: Class 415/1 No 5224 forms a Slade Green to Cannon Street via Bexleyheath service on 7 June 1976. It is seen here taking the Cannon Street line at Borough Market Junction. *Brian Morrison*

Below: Blue and grey livery is becoming ever more widely applied. Class 415/1 No 5263 has also been internally refurbished, and was photographed on 28 September 1979 leaving Waterloo on a train for Guildford via Cobham. Sister unit No 5131 on the right will shortly be leaving for Hampton Court. *John Glover*

Far left: The 2SAP units were created by downclassing former 2HAP units. Conversion consisted of the simple expedient of removing the antimacassars and carpets in the first class compartments, together with all indications of their former status. Class 418/1 No 5906 enters Chertsey with the Weybridge to Staines shuttle on 7 September 1977. *John Glover*

Left: On 24 August 1979 4BEP Class 410/2 unit No 7021 emerges from Shakespeare Cliff Tunnel at Dover with a Boat Train from Victoria. *John Glover*

Below left: Class 411/2 No 7171 forms the 18.12 Margate to Charing Cross on 28 May 1977, and is seen

here entering Canterbury West. On the left, Class 423 No 7875 departs for Margate, having left London as the 16.55 from Victoria, via Maidstone. *Wyn Hobson*

Above: The 11.08 Dover Marine to Victoria formed of Class 419 Motor Luggage Van No 68005 and 4CEP unit Class 411/2 No 7146 passes Snowdown & Nonington on 4 April 1975. *Wyn Hobson*

Below: 4CIG Class 421/1 No 7323 leaves Hastings on the last stage of the journey from Victoria to Ore on 16 October 1978. *John Glover*

Above left: A Victoria to Brighton express service leaves Quarry Tunnel on 4 September 1979. The leading unit is Class 421/1 No 7302.   *John Glover*

Centre left: In the New Forest at Sway, 4REP Class 430 unit No 3002 is seen on an up Bournemouth to Waterloo semi-fast service in May 1977. *John Glover*

Below : At Sway on the down line, 4VEP Class 423 unit No 7818 nears the end of its (nearly) all stations journey from Waterloo to Bournemouth in March 1978.   *John Glover*

Right: Under the magnificent overall roof at Brighton, Class 423 unit No 7797 waits to depart with a semi-fast service to Portsmouth Harbour on 16 September 1977. *John Glover*

Below right: Latterly, some 4VEP units have been converted to 4VEG stock by removing some seating bays and thus creating more luggage space. Intended for the Gatwick services, they have been suitably emblazoned; Class 427 unit No 7909 leaves Victoria on 17 September 1979. *John Glover*

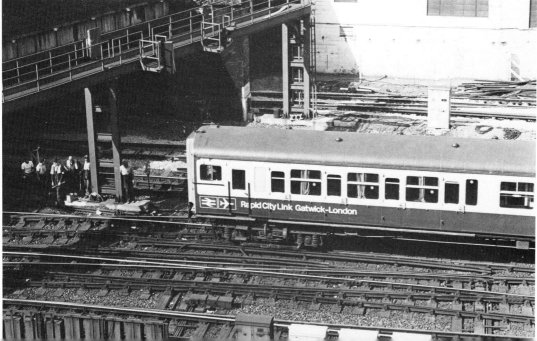

Right: The conventional view of Bank station with prewar Class 487 car No S54 leading on arrival on 8 December 1979. The letter 'A' displayed on the front of the train denotes the diagram on which the train is working, and is not a headcode. *Brian Morrison*

Below: On arrival at Waterloo, trains run forward into the sidings before reversing into the departure platform. Class 487 car No S52 is the leading vehicle. *Brian Morrison*

The Industrials

And finally ... English Electric built for many other concerns in the United Kingdom apart from British Rail. Some of these customers were industrial firms with their own railway systems, and four standard gauge examples are illustrated here. The locomotives form part of the 'Stephenson' range, which is available in various gauges and with 0-4-0 or 0-6-0 wheel arrangements.

Industrial locomotive manufacture was, and indeed still is, carried out at Vulcan Foundry. Key points in the design are simplicity and accessibility for ease of maintenance. To ensure safety of working conditions, a recess is available at each corner of the locomotive to enable shunting staff to ride within the loading gauge. Despite the success of the diesel electric shunter on BR, many of the industrial applications use hydraulic transmission because of the sizeable savings in initial costs. All the locomotives depicted use Dorman engines and Twin Disc Torque Converters.

Below; A pair of English Electric 0-6-0s shunt at British Steel Corporation's Corby works on 29 September 1977. *Kevin Lane*

Left: 0-6-0 diesel hydraulic APG No 1 (English Electric Vulcan D1138 of 1966) sits in the sun at NCB Aberpergwm Colliery, Glyn Neath, West Glamorgan on 6 April 1978.   *Kevin Lane*

Below: No D4 (English Electric Vulcan D1195 of 1967) takes waste colliery material empties from dumping at the southern end of the system at Seaham Harbour, County Durham, back to the bottom of the NCB incline. From here they will return via the rope to South Hetton Colliery. The date is 30 June 1978.   *Kevin Lane*

Bottom: 0-6-0 diesel-hydraulic No 3 (English Electric Vulcan D1228 of 1967) pauses between duties at CEGB Hams Hall power station, Coleshill, Birmingham in August 1977.   *Kevin Lane.*